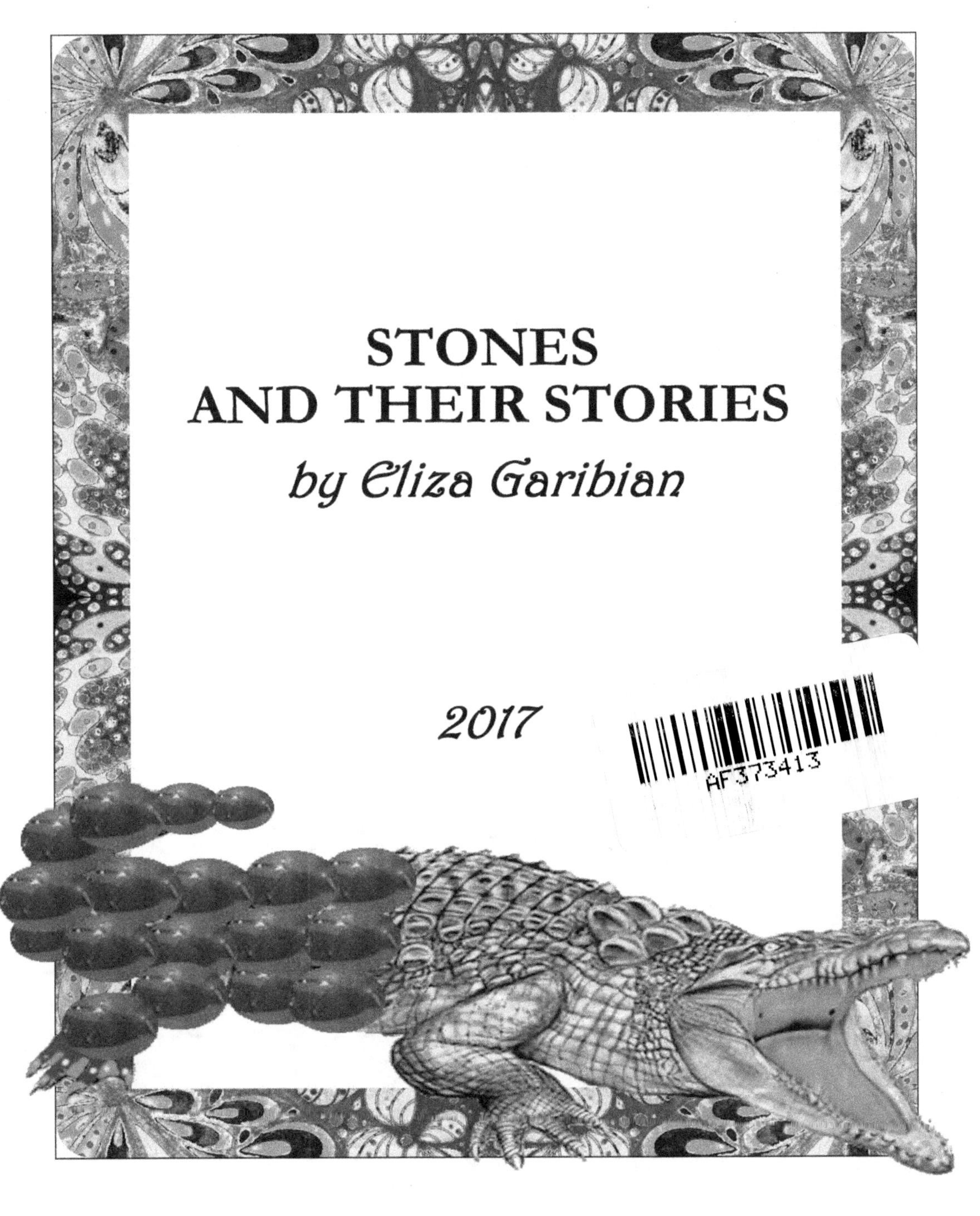

STONES
AND THEIR STORIES

by Eliza Garibian

2017

CONTENTS

I adore wearing gems, but not because they are mine. You can't possess radiance, you can only admire it.

Elizabeth Taylor

PREFACE

All stones, being that gemstones or scenic rock formations, seem to hold a mystery inside, and people, starting from long time ago, have created numerous stories and legends about them.

Because precious stones are highly priced, the most expensive ones were many times stolen, men were killed, and jewels passed from one owner to another.

In this book, you will read remarkable facts about stones, their stories and explanation of the origin of their names. Also, you will find common beliefs in talismanic values of the described gems and information about your birthstone.

From ancient times, India was the main source of jewels – no wonder interesting gemstone myths originated there. Here is the one, recounting creation of gemstones.

According to the legend, Indian Gods decided to get rid of demon Vala. They united and killed him, chopped and threw his body parts on the Earth. The demon's body was purified during the sacrifice and his body parts became gems. Drops of the blood transformed into **rubies**, his skin turned into yellow **sapphires**, eyes became blue **sapphires** and his bones shattered into **diamonds**. The teeth fell into the oceans and landed on oysters where they became **pearls**. Vala's intestines, thrown into the sea, turned into **corals**. His bright green bile became **emeralds** and his fat turned into **jade** or **quartz**. Finally, even Vala's last cry that echoed around the heavens was transformed into **cat's eyes**.

As we can see from this story, gemstones were associated with different body parts and ancient people used them to cure corresponding parts of the human body.

Another amazing fact about jewels is that they were said to have sex. The darker varieties were regarded as being male and the lighter ones as female. Moreover, some writers of stories about jewels, declared that certain gems were capable of producing offspring.

As an example, they say that the pearl-fishers of Indonesia preserved every ninth **pearl** and placed them in a bottle with two grains of rice for each pearl, believing that these pearls have the power to breed others. On top of that, custom required to have a finger of a dead man as a plug for this bottle.

In the Old Testament **High Priest of the Israelites, Aaron**, was described wearing a breastplate with twelve gemstones (there is Aaron's sculpture with the breastplate in the Santa Maria del Rosario Church in Venice, Italy). Each stone was representing a specific tribe, whose name was inscribed on the stone. Each tribe was associated with the zodiac sign. Thus, birthstones were defined.

Ancient people believed that wearing talismans, birthstones and zodiac gems would protect a person from the evil spirits. Each month had its stone, and it was recommended to wear stones corresponding to the month to maximize the gem's therapeutic and talismanic virtues.

Everybody knows about faceted gemstones, but not many have heard the name of an alternate gem-shaping technique: **cabochon.**

The word comes from the French word "*caboche*", meaning "head". Cabochon form of the gemstone usually has a rounded front with a flat reverse side.

While faceting is usually applied to transparent stones, cabochon is used for modeling opaque gems.

After reading this book you'll also know about **zircon** and **cubic zirconia**, which sound alike but are completely different stones. You'll learn about **"mystic"** stones, **rhinestones**, **fianit** and what is hidden under the name of **Roman Glass** (RG) that is used in the jewelry.

If you are finding any of the mentioned above topics interesting, **THIS BOOK IS FOR YOU!**

AGATE

 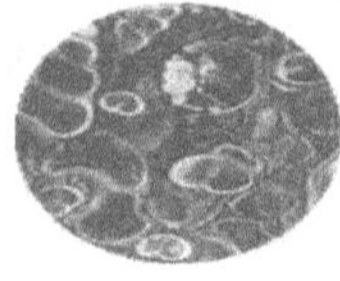 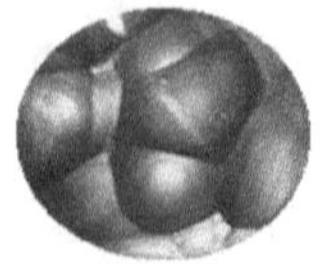 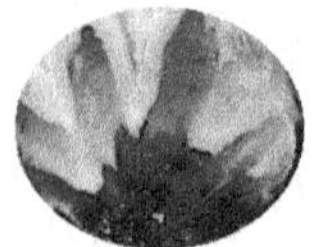

The name "agate" (агат, ագատ) comes from the Greek word for the river Achates, in Sicily, where the mineral was found in significant quantities.

Agate is a variety of **chalcedony**. It is one of the first materials known to man.

There are different kinds of agate: **moss** or dendritic agate, **turritella** agate, formed from silicified fossil shells, **fire** agate, **Coyamito** agate from Mexico, **banded agate**, which exhibits succession of parallel lines, and more. First four of the above mentioned stones are represented in the pictures in the same sequence.

According to the legends, agate makes the wearer agreeable and persuasive. It is also said to cure insomnia and give to its owner pleasant dreams.

ALEXANDRITE

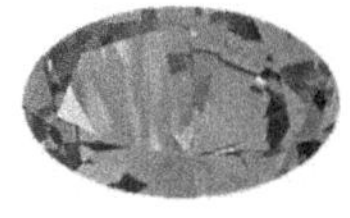

A relatively modern gem, alexandrite (александрит, ալեքսանդրիտ) was discovered in Russian emerald mines located in the Ural Mountains.

Legend claims that it was discovered in 1834, on the same day that future Russian Czar, Alexander II, came of age, hence the name honoring him.

Because this unique gemstone changes colors from green to red—the national colors of Russia—alexandrite became Imperial Russia's official gemstone.

Often described as "emerald by day, ruby by night," alexandrite is a rare variety of the **chrysoberyl** which changes color from **bluish green** in daylight to **purplish red** under electric light.

Alexandrite is said to harmonize its owner's feelings, increases happiness and the power of imagination.

AMBER

The name "amber" (янтарь, ишр) is derived from the Arabic "*anbar*", possibly meaning "dew fallen from the sky". Ancient Greeks called amber "electron" meaning "beaming sun". The word "electricity" actually originated from this word.

Amber is fossilized tree resin. Sometimes it contains inclusions of animal and plant material.

Here is an old Greek legend about amber.

Once Phaeton, the son of Helios—the god of Sun, decided to try his father's job. He convinced Helios to allow him to drive the Sun Chariot across the sky for a day.

However the horses, feeling the inexperienced hands of Phaeton, went out of control. For some time they steered the Sun Chariot too far away from the Earth, and the Earth became very cold. Then they went too close to the Earth and burned parts of it. In order to save the entire planet from burning, Zeus had no choice but to strike Phaeton down with one of his lightning bolts.

Phaeton fell dead into the Eridanus River.

Learning of his death, Phaeton's grieving sisters came to the river and wept day and night for their dead brother. After some time, their bodies turned into poplar trees. Their tears, however, continued to flow, and as they hardened in the sun, they turned into amber.

There is a lot of amber on the shores of the Baltic Sea. The Baltic amber is associated with the Lithuanian legend about Juratė, the queen of the sea, who lived in a beautiful Palace of Amber.

Unfortunately, she was destined to fall in love with Kastytis, a plain fisherman. Learning that, her frustrated father punished his daughter by destroying her Palace of Amber and transforming Juratė into sea foam.

From that day on, people started finding amber on the Baltic coastline — those were the pieces of the once beautiful Amber Palace.

Another famous story related to amber is a story of Amber Room in the Catherine Palace, near St. Petersburg, Russia. The room was considered the "Eighth wonder of the world". It was decorated in amber panels and, initially, built by the order of the Prussian king.

After some time, the Room was gifted to **Peter the Great of Russia**, which forged a Russian-Prussian alliance against Sweden.

In Russia, by the order of **Empress Catherine II**, the daughter of Peter the Great, the Amber Room was enlarged and enriched with gold plated wooden carvings, mirrors and mosaic pictures of agate and jasper.

However, During World War II the Amber Room disappeared, and, until now, just parts of it reappear from time to time.

There are numerous theories of its possible whereabouts.

It may have been secretly transferred by the Nazis to South Africa and is in the hands of their descendants. Or it was secretly transported to the USA, where it is now in private collections.

Other possibilities include that it may have been buried under the ground or has been burned down.

In 2003 the Amber Room was recreated, and some say it now looks even better than the original one.

As a stone, amber is believed to be a powerful healer that gives the person who wears it a sense of health. It helps to balance emotions, clear the mind and release negative energy.

AMETHYST

The name "amethyst" (аметист, մեղեսիկ) comes from the Greek word "*methustos*," which means "intoxicated."

Amethyst is a **violet** variety of **quartz**.

According to the Greek myth, one day Dionysus, the god of wine and intoxication, became angry with the mortals and decided he would have revenge by letting his two tigers devour the next human he sees.

Unfortunately, a beautiful young virgin named Amethysta was the first one who caught his sight. She was on her way to Diana's temple to pay homage to the goddess of the Moon, hunt and nature.

The furious god unleashed his hungry tigers upon her. Terrified Amethysta cried out to Diana for help. When goddess Diana saw what was about to happen, she turned Amethysta into a statue of gleaming clear quartz, protecting her from the tigers.

As the time passed, Dionysus realized the cruelty of his action. He began to weep tears over the statue of Amethysta. But his tears were of wine and stained the quartz statue in beautiful purple color. This is how the stone called amethyst was created.

It is believed that amethyst could protect the owner from drunkenness.

10
AQUAMARINE

The name "aquamarine" (аквамарин, ծովական) is derived from the Latin word "*aqua*", meaning water, and "*marina*", meaning the sea.

Aquamarine, together with **emerald**, is a variety of **beryl**.

In the Middle Ages, many believed that the simple act of wearing aquamarine was a literal antidote to poisoning.

The Romans thought that if you carved a frog into a piece of aquamarine jewelry, it would help to reconcile differences between enemies and make new friends.

It is also said that aquamarine is Neptune's gift to the mermaids.

This gemstone was believed to protect sailors, as well as to guarantee a safe voyage.

The **pale blue** or **blue-green** color of aquamarine is said to cool one's temper, allowing the wearer to remain calm and levelheaded.

BERYL

Beryl (берилл, բերիլիում) is a mineral that possibly got its name from the Greek "*beryllos*", named after Indian city Belur, known for its **emeralds,** a variety of **beryl**.

Pure beryl is colorless, but it is frequently tinted by impurities. Existing colors are **green, blue, yellow, red, pink** and **white**.

Here are some of varieties of beryl: aquamarine, **heliodor** "gift of sun", morganite, also known as **"pink beryl"**, named after American financier and famous gem collector J.P. Morgan.

CARNELIAN

The "carnelian" name (сердолик, սարդիոն) comes from the Latin word "*cornum*", the "cornel cherry" - a plant in the dogwood family, the red fruits of which resemble the stone.

Carnelian is a brownish-red mineral, a variety of **chalcedony**.

A stone similar to the carnelian is **sard,** with generally darker color, as well as **sardonyx –** red shaded onyx. All these stones were popular stones for Roman seals and signet rings that were used to imprint wax emblems on official documents—due to the fact that hot wax doesn't stick to this stone.

An Armenian writer of the 17th century writes about how wearing a carnelian can save one from injury, especially emphasizing, "No man who wore a carnelian was ever found in a collapsed house or beneath a fallen wall," - words from a person apparently well acquainted with earthquakes, which are frequent in Armenia.

Wearing a carnelian is recommended to those who are timid in speech, for the warm-colored stone will give them the courage they lack.

CAT'S EYE

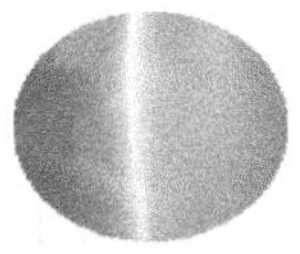

Cat's eye (кошачий глаз, կատվի աչք), or **cymophane** is a variety of **chrysoberyl**. It is a **yellowish chatoyant**.

Chatoyant is a stone which visually resembles cat's eye.

The word "chatoyant" comes from the French *"œil de chat"*, meaning "cat's eye", effect also seen in the gem called **tiger's eye**.

Another stone that is promoted as tiger's eye from Namibia and China is **pietersite**.

Wearing cat's eye is believed to help return lost wealth, bring good luck to gamblers and protect from the evil eye.

CHALCEDONY

The name "chalcedony" (халцедон, խալցեդոն) comes from the Latin *"chalcedonius"* derived from the town Chalcedon, from where the mineral came from, and located on a small peninsula near the mouth of the Bosphorus.

Chalcedony may be semitransparent or translucent and comes in wide range of colors. Here are famous varieties of chalcedony: **agate**, **carnelian**, **chrysoprase**, **heliotrope**, **jasper** and **onyx**.

CHRYSOBERYL

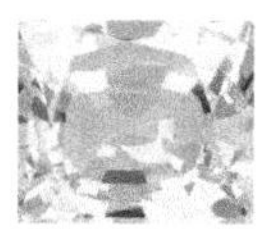

The name "chrysoberyl" (хризоберилл, խրիզոբերիլ) is derived from the Greek "chrysos beryllos", meaning "a gold beryl".

The ordinary chrysoberyl has a **yellow-to-green** color. The more expensive kinds of chrysoberyl are **cat's eye** and **alexandrite**.

Chrysoberyl is believed to protect the wearer from the evil eye.

CHRYSOPRASE

The name "chrysoprase" (хризопраз, ηυկեզμρηιխυυ) comes from the Greek "*chrysos*" meaning "gold" and "*prasinon*" meaning "green".

Chrysoprase is a variety of **chalcedony**. It comes in different varieties. The best ones are colored in homogenous **emerald-green** and **granny smith apple green** bright colors.

Chrysoprase was the favorite stone of **Frederick the Great**, the King of Prussia. His palace at Potsdam, Germany, named Sanssouci ("*sans souci*" means "carefree" in French) had many objects of furniture made of chrysoprase. Palace became a World Heritage Site and is protected by UNESCO.

Frederick the Great's father, known as the "king-soldier" was the one who presented the Amber Room to Peter the Great of Russia, to get an ally against Sweden.

CITRINE

The name "citrine" (цитрин, ghunphû) is derived from the Latin word "*citrina*", which means "yellow" and is also the origin of the word "citron".

Citrine is a variety of **quartz**. Brazil is the largest supplier of citrine.

Sometimes citrine and amethyst can be found together in the same crystal, which is then referred to as **ametrine**.

Citrine stone is known as "healing quartz" for its ability to comfort, soothe and calm. It can alleviate negative feelings and spark imagination.

It is also called the "merchant's stone" for its tendency to attract wealth and prosperity.

CORAL

The Greek word for coral (коралл, մարջան) is "gorgeia" sounding similar to "Gorgon".

According to the legend, coral originated because of the magical effect of Gorgon Medusa. Medusa was a winged human female monster, with poisonous snakes in place of hair. Any living creature, who gazed at her face, was turned to stone.

Perseus was a Greek hero who succeeded in cutting Medusa's head.

It is said that Perseus, while washing his hands, placed Medusa's head on the riverbank. When he picked it up again, he saw that her blood had transformed seaweed into red coral.

Those were the first ever seen corals and hence their Greek name.

Although until the eighteenth century people believed corals to be plants, they are actually animals.

The corals that are widely used in jewelry are called "precious" or "red" corals. They have durable and intensely colored red or pink skeletons.

Also very valued is jewelry from the black corals. Black coral is the official state gem of Hawaii.

Coral ornaments were found in ancient burials throughout the world.

In Italy coral was worn to protect from the evil eye, and by women as a cure for infertility. It was thought to guard children from harm and treat wounds from bites of snakes and scorpions.

DIAMOND

The name "diamond" (бриллиант, ադամանդ) is derived from the Greek "*adamas*" – "unbreakable", "untamed".

Here is a legend about creation of the diamond.

One day the God of the Mines ordered to bring him all known gems. He took one of each kind, crushed and mixed them all together. Then he made a diamond out of the mix and said, "Let this jewel be pure like a drop of dew, combine the beauty of all the gemstones and be invincible in hardness."

It is said that arrows of Cupid, the god of desire, are tipped with diamonds, which bring magic of love to the hearts they pierce. This is one of the reasons that diamonds are a popular stone for engagement rings.

Many tales are told about the most precious diamonds.

Among them are the **Orlov** and **Shah** diamonds, both now in the collection of the **Diamond Fund of Russia**, in Moscow Kremlin. Here are their stories.

According to the legend, the Orlov diamond, was initially one of the diamonds in the eyes of the statue of Brahma, in a temple in Madras, India.

The diamond was stolen by a French soldier and, after changing hands for several times, was bought by Count Orlov, who presented it to **Empress Catherine the Great** of Russia, hoping to get back in her favor (read Comments on p. 54 for alternate story). Although, he didn't succeed in that, the diamond was named after him. It is a very big gem, in the shape and proportions resembling half of a chicken's egg.

The Shah Diamond was found in Indian mines in the 15th century and belonged to the Indian rulers until it was seized by the Persian Shah, who attacked India, and brought the diamond to Persia. There it stayed for almost a century until 1829.

That year, Russian embassy in Teheran, headed by ambassador **Griboedov**, a famous Russian writer, was sheltering in its building Armenians – two women that escaped from the harem, and an eunuch, who, according to the Shah's believes, knew too much.

Armenians were asking Griboedov to help them to return to Armenia, which at that time became part of Russia. The Islamists demanded return of fugitives but Griboedov denied them. That caused anger among fanatics, who attacked the Russian embassy and, despite resistance, slaughtered everybody, including ambassador Griboedov.

Therefore, to smooth aggravated diplomatic conflict between countries, Persia sent Shah's grandson with rich gifts for the Russian Tsar. Among the gifts was the Shah Diamond.

The body of A. Griboedov was sent to Georgia where it was buried in a monastery in Tbilisi.

From the words of famous Russian poet A.S. **Pushkin** we know, that while traveling in Armenia, he, by chance, came upon men from Teheran leading an oxcart with the remains of the ambassador.

There is a monument in Dilijan, Armenia, commemorating the location where this encounter of two great Russian writers Pushkin and Griboedov, who never met during the life of Griboedov, took place.

Another famous diamond is **Koh-i-Noor** (meaning Mountain of Light). It changed hands several times among different rulers of South Asia, but after conquer of Punjab by Britain, it was presented to Queen Victoria.

17

EMERALD

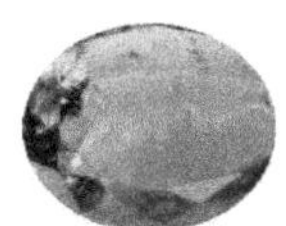

The name "emerald" (изумруд, զմրուխտ) is from the Greek word "*smaragdus*," that means "green". It is a well-known variety of **beryl**.

Cleopatra is perhaps the most famous historical figure to cherish emeralds. Hers were the mines of Egypt.

On the other side of the world, the Muzo Indians of Colombia also had emerald mines. These mines were so well hidden, it took the Spanish conquistadors nearly twenty years to find them.

A long time ago, the people of the Peruvian city of Manta worshipped an emerald the size of an ostrich egg, which they called goddess Umina. Her priests brought Umina out of the temple only on special days. According to them, her followers should worship "the mother emerald" by bringing her "daughters," smaller emeralds, to her.

When the Spaniards conquered the town, they seized a big amount of "daughter" emeralds. However, they never found the carefully hidden "mother".

There is an ancient Colombian legend about the origin of emeralds.

Fura and Tena were ancestors of Colombians. The god Ares created them to be immortal. However, to possess eternal youth, they had to remain faithful to each other, a condition that was broken by Fura, the woman, who fell in love with a blond stranger.

As a punishment, Ares took away their immortality. Both aged rapidly, and when they died, they were transformed into two pointing hills – Fura and Tena. They say that the tears of Fura turned into emeralds and butterflies.

Today, the Fura and Tena peaks rising above the valley of the Minero River, are the guardians of Colombia's emerald zone.

Emerald is considered a stone of hope and love.

FELDSPAR

The name "feldspar" (полевой шпат, դաշտային շպատ) derives from the German *"feldspat"* where *"feld"* means field and *"spat"* – a rock that does not contain metal.

Feldspar is the most common mineral on the Earth. It can be of **pink, white, gray, green** and **brown** colors.

Recently, feldspar was found on the Moon and Mars.

Labradorite, moonstone, **amazonite** (greenish stone) and **sunstone** are examples of feldspar.

FLUORITE

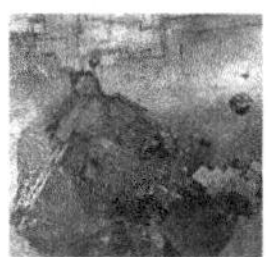

The name "fluorite" (флюорит, ֆլյուորիտ) is derived from the Latin verb *"fluere"* meaning "to flow" because of its low melting point.

In 1852 it gave its name to the phenomenon of **fluorescence**, which is seen in many fluorites, because of impurities in the crystals.

Fluorites absorb ultraviolet radiation and emit light in visible spectrum, which gives fluorites distinct colors. Fluorescence stops, once UV radiation is stopped.

Fluorites can have all colors of the rainbow, plus **black** and **white**. The most common colors are **purple**, **blue**, **green**, **yellow**, and colorless.

The best known fluorite is the purple-blue mineral, called "**Blue John**".

It is widely used as an ornament and was discovered in England in the eighteenth century. Among many explanations of the name origin, the popular one is that it comes from the French *"bleu-jaune"*, meaning "blue-yellow".

During World War I, two cups made of "Blue John" mineral were discovered in Roman burials. That showed that ancients also were familiar with this rock.

After that discovery it became obvious that the cups mentioned by Roman writers as beautifully carved from attractive rock, which they called *murrhine*, were "Blue John" cups. They were described as giving a pleasing taste to wine drunk from them. This was probably from the residual myrrh that was applied to the stones, while they were carved.

Both cups, called the Barber Cup and the Crawford Cup, are now in the collection of the **British Museum**.

Fluorite may be used in jewelry, but due to its softness, it is mostly used for ornamental carvings.

GARNET

The word "garnet" (гранат, նռնաքար) comes from the 14th Century Middle English word "*gernet*" meaning dark red, which in its turn comes from the Latin "*granatum*" possibly referring to the pomegranate.

The name **carbuncle** is also used for **any** red gemstone, most often a red garnet. There is also gem called **almandine,** a garnet with **deep red color**, inclining to **purple**.

Garnet is believed to give power and authority to the wearer. Also, it can instill strong and passionate desire.

HELIOTROPE

The name "heliotrope" (гелиотроп, հելիոտրոպ) comes from the Greek words "*helios*" and "*trepein*", meaning "turning the sun", because it was believed that this stone could affect the sun and steer the weather, causing thunder, lightning and rain.

Heliotrope is a variety of **chalcedony**. It is also known as "**bloodstone**" because of the red inclusions that resemble spots of blood.

Other names of the stone are "stone of Babylon" and "Stephan's stone".

In ancient times it was used to stop bleeding. Christians made church utensils from heliotrope, trusting in its powerful healing energy.

This stone is believed to be a "helper", not a "stimulant". It will not make you work but will increase your productivity and help in your studies.

JADE

The English word "jade" (нефрит, նեֆրիտ) is derived from the Spanish term "*piedra de ijada*" or "loin stone", from its reputed efficacy in curing ailments of the loins and kidneys.

Another word used for jade is "nephrite", derived from "*lapis nephriticus*", a Latin translation of the Spanish "*piedra de ijada*".

The term "jade" is applied to two different rocks: **nephrite** and **jadeite**.

Nephrite can be found in **white** color and in **light green**.

Jadeite can be **blue**, **lavender**, pink and **emerald green**. Jadeite is a rarer stone of the two. Burma and Guatemala are the principal sources of modern jadeite.

The Chinese called jade the "stone of life" and valued it often above gold and silver. Jade is their national stone. According to Chinese legends, the Phoenix and the Dragon are the source of life of family clans, and their symbols are often carved on ornaments from jade.

An ancient Chinese proverb says, "Gold has a price, jade is priceless." Confucius spoke of a good man: "His morals are pure, like jade."

The Jade Prince is a collective name for several archaeological finds from the elite burials of ancient China. The bodies of the people were completely decayed, but the funeral garments, that were made from thousand pieces of jade, connected to each other with golden wire, are preserved.

Jade is believed to promote wisdom, balance and peace.

JASPER

The name "jasper" (яшма, հшuująchu) is derived from Semitic language word *"yashupo"* that means "spotted stone".

Jasper is an opaque patterned rock of virtually any color. It was a favorite gem in the ancient world, where in many cases it was distinctly **green** and resembled **jade**.

In old times jasper was used in seals and signet rings.

Jasper is known as a stone of gentleness, comfort and relaxation. It is sometimes called the "nurturing stone".

JET

The English name "jet" (гагат, qшqшıп) is derived from the French name for this stone: "*jaiet*", while Russian name uses the Latin name for the stone "gagate".

The adjective "jet-black", meaning the darkest black, comes from the dark black color of this stone.

Jet is predecessor of coal and is a gemstone. It is a product of high-pressure decomposition of wood from millions of years ago.

Jet artifacts are known from as early as 10,000 BC.

Legend says that this gem is the **amber** of witches. It was an old tradition among the wives of fishermen to burn small pieces of jet on the beach to ensure the return of their men with a good catch.

Jet was frequently used in amulets and pendants because it was believed to deflect the gaze of the evil eye. Because of its color, it was associated with mourning jewelry and often fashioned into rosaries for monks.

In the 1920-ies, in the times of Art Nouveaux, it was popular to wear multiple strands of jet beads stretching from the neckline to the waistline. Unlike black glass, which is cool to the touch, jet is warm.

Ebonite (a brand name for very hard rubber) looks like jet but fades over time.

Anthracite has been used to imitate jet. The name "anthracite" is derived from the Greek word meaning "coal-like".

Anthracite was used in furnaces to heat buildings. Because the fuel was smokeless, it was used in the American Civil War by Confederate steam ships bringing supplies of guns, in order to not to give away their position.

Jet is thought to ease anxiety and depression.

LABRADORITE

Labradorite (лабрадорит, լաբրադորիտ) was discovered on the coast of Labrador – the northern region of Canada.

There is an Inuit legend about it. Word "Inuit" means "the People" in the language of Aborigines (they are better known as Eskimos, the Native American word that means "the eaters of raw meat").

Legend says that long ago, the Northern Lights fell from the sky and were trapped inside some rocks off the coast of Labrador.

One day, an Inuit warrior came to these rocks and tried to set the Northern Lights free. With blows from his spear, he was able to release most of the lights, but some remained permanently stuck within the rocks.

It is said that trapped Northern Lights are what give the labradorite its brilliant flashes of light and color.

Labradorite is considered to clear, balance and protect the aura, and gives general protection to the owner.

LAPIS LAZULI

"*Lapis*" comes from the Latin word meaning "stone" and "*lazuli*" comes from Persian "*lajavard*" which means "blue stone", and is the name of the place in Persia where lapis lazuli (лазурит, լաջվարդ) was mined.

The stone is also known as **lazurite**.

Lazurite is a member of the **sodalite** group. It has **deep blue** to **greenish blue** color. Sodalite itself is a rich **royal blue** mineral with white veins.

In ancient Egypt, lapis lazuli, together with **jasper**, **amethyst** and **carnelian**, was a favorite stone for amulets and ornaments like **scarabs**.

Scarabs are called talismans carved or molded in the form of a scarab beetle.

Lazurite was believed to be a powerful stone that helps connect to God. That is why the High Priests colored themselves and their garments with a special mix made of the crushed lazurite.

As another example of the belief in power of lapis lazuli, there is a legend, saying that **King Solomon** had a ring of lazurite, with which he controlled an army of demons, helping him in building his First Temple in Jerusalem. It is interesting to know, that according to the same legend, Solomon's artisans used **Shamir worm** in place of cutting tools.

Shamir is a mythic worm or substance that had the power to cut through stone, iron or wood. It was used because the First Temple was to promote Peace, so it was thought inappropriate to use tools with which it was possible to kill.

Lazurite mines of Afghanistan are the oldest ones. The stones from these mines were discovered in the tombs of pharaohs and during the excavation of Troy.

Lapis lazuli is known as "Afghanistan's Blue Treasure" and is considered the second important source of income of the Taliban.

During the Renaissance period, lapis was ground and made into pigment ultramarine for use in frescoes and oil painting.

Lapis lazuli is considered a universal symbol of wisdom and truth.

LIMESTONE

Limestone (известняк, կրաքար) is a **sedimentary** rock, composed mostly of skeletal fragments of marine organisms (corals, molluscs). Its main use is as a building material.

Often the bands of limestone emerge from the Earth's surface as spectacular rocky boulders and islands.

One of the beautiful examples of limestone formations are the numerous islets in the Ha Long Bay, Vietnam. Ha Long translated from Vietnamese means "descending dragon". This name originated because of the numerous appearances in the bay of a giant sea snake, which resembled an Asian dragon.

LOADSTONE

In Middle English "loadstone" (магнитный железняк) means "course stone". It is a naturally magnetized piece of the mineral magnetite. It can attract iron. Loadstones were used in compasses when they were first created.

There is a theory that loadstones are magnetized by the strong magnetic fields surrounding lightning bolts.

The name "magnet" may come from the loadstones found in Magnesia, Anatolia.

MALACHITE

The name (малахит, մալախիտ) is derived from the Greek "*molochitis lithos*", meaning "malva-green stone" for resemblance to the leaves of the plant "*moloche*" – malva.

Large amounts of malachite are located in the Ural Mountains in Russia.

Emperor Nicholas I had a malachite room, with malachite-coated walls in the Winter Palace, Saint Petersburg.

There is a famous book "The Malachite Box" by P. Bazhov, which includes fairy tales of the Ural Mountain miners about the Mistress of the Copper Mountain and her amazing gardens of gemstones.

One of the stories is about a young stone-craftsman who made beautiful vases of stone but was never satisfied with the quality of his own work. After hearing the myth that the most beautiful Malachite Stone Flower was in the possession of the Mistress of the Copper Mountain, the young man decided to see the Flower despite of all the mysteries surrounding its Mistress.

According to one of them, for those, who see the Stone Flower, life loses sweetness and they become the Mistress' stone craftsmen forever.

Nevertheless, the young man left his home and fiancé, and went to the mountains. For two years, nobody heard from him. Then, one day, he came back, destroyed all his craft, and disappeared forever.

Some people say that he lost his mind and died somewhere in the woods, but others say that the Mistress of the Mountain has taken him to work for her.

Malachite is said to protect the wearer from accidents and helps to succeed in business.

MOLDAVITE

"Vltavin" is the Czech name for the stone better known as **"moldavite"** (молдавит, մոլդավիտ).

The name is derived from the name of Czech town *"Tyn nad Vltavou"* and *"Moldauthein"* is the German name for that same town, from where the first samples of **moldavite** came.

They were discovered in the eighteenth century. In the beginning of 20th century, there was a theory that moldavite was a type of meteorite.

Currently, the majority of scientists believe that moldavite was formed some 14.7 million years ago as a result of the collision of a giant meteorite with Earth in the area of southern Germany.

Pieces of earth material that were melted because of high temperatures generated during the impact, were thrown in the air where they cooled down and fell back to the ground mostly in the region of Bohemia in a form of moldavite we know.

Substances like moldavite were discovered also in other parts of the world near craters left by meteorite impacts. They were called **tektites** and have black, green (moldavite), brown or gray colors.

In 1960, another non-terrestrial hypothesis for the origin of tektites was proposed. According to it, tektites were formed as a result of nuclear blasts produced by extraterrestrial beings.

Moldavite belongs to the category of glass and can be transparent with an olive-green color and with bubbles. High quality stones are often used in jewelry.

Another glass that is used in jewelry is **Roman Glass**. In this jewelry, instead of stones, the pieces of broken artifacts discovered in Roman excavations are used.

MOONSTONE

The name "moonstone" (лунный камень, լուսնաքար) originated because of its shine resembling moonlight, caused by light diffraction in the stone.

The Romans admired moonstone, as they believed it was born from solidified rays of the moon. In their mythology moonstone was the stone of Diana, the goddess of the moon.

The moonstone is considered to enhance feminine energies, psychic abilities and protect women during pregnancy and childbirth.

It is also known as the traveler's stone because it is assumed to protect those travelling at night time or by sea.

Deposits of moonstone occur also in Armenia, mainly from the mines near Lake Sevan.

OBSIDIAN

 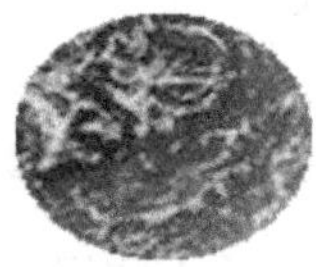

Roman explorer Obsidius was the one who discovered obsidian (обсидиан, օբսիդիան, վանակատ), a natural volcanic glass, in Ethiopia, hence the name.

There is a legend about small rounded obsidian rocks with grayish-white dots, called "Apache tears".

In Arizona, after a bloody conflict between Apaches and settlers, white men surrounded the last surviving Apache warriors. Rather than die at the hands of white men, these last warriors chose death by leaping over the cliff's edge. The Apache women gathered at the base of the cliff, and wept for their dead. They mourned, not only because their warriors had all died, but also because the fighting spirit of the Apaches had died with them. Their sadness was so immense that the Great Spirit encased the tears of the Apache women into black stones we now call Apache tears.

Ancient people used obsidian to make tools, knives, mirrors and decorative objects. On Easter Island, it was used as pupils for the eyes of Moai human figures.

Armenians often call this stone **"devil's nail"** and here is why. Cain and Abel were sons of Adam and Eve. Cain was jealous of his brother and decided to kill him but didn't know how. Suddenly the devil appeared in a form of a black crow and pointed Cain to a piece of obsidian. Cain used obsidian as a knife to kill his brother and after that, obsidian got its name: "devil's nail" (սատանի եղունգ).

Obsidian is considered excellent for removing negativity and giving protection against psychic attacks.

ONYX

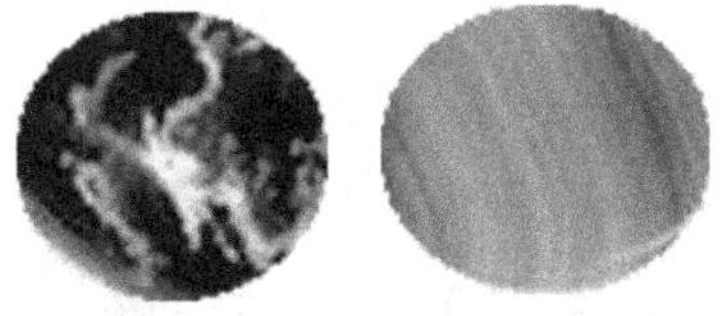

The name "onyx" (оникс, օնիքս) comes from the Greek word meaning "fingernail" or "claw". It is a variety of **chalcedony**. Here is its story.

Venus, the goddess of love and beauty, was resting by a river when her son, Cupid, came along and used the diamond point of one of his enchanted arrows to give his mother a manicure while she slept.

With the nail clippings in his hands, he joyfully flew up into the sky, but with all of his excitement, he accidentally dropped the clippings and they fell into the river.

Immediately, Venus' nail clippings turned into onyx.

Onyx consists of bands of chalcedony of different colors.

There is also **sardonyx** "red onyx", which has **red** colored bands.

There are also **yellow** and **green** varieties of onyx, used for interior decoration of palaces and theaters (like walls of yellow onyx in Mariinsky Theatre in St. Petersburg).

Onyx stone is used for protection, improvement of relationship between couples, support in difficult times.

OPAL

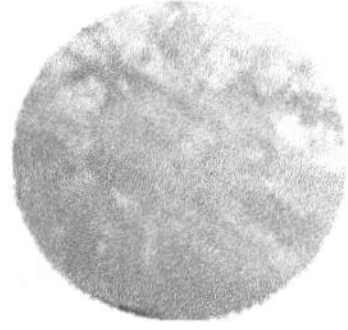

The name "opal" (опал, օպալ)originates from the Greek word "*opallios*", which means "to see a change in color."

The Roman scholar Pliny used the word "*opalus*" when he wrote about this gem's kaleidoscopic "play" of colors that could simulate shades of any stone.

Australia is rich in opal mines. Australian Aborigines have created many stories about this stone. According to one of them, their ancestor came to earth by a great rainbow, and, at the place where the rainbow rested, there appeared a big area of rocks that glitter in the sun with a variety of colors. These rocks were opals.

According to an Arabic legend, opals fell from the sky in bolts of lightning.

These days there is a man-made opal simulate, that is called **opalite**.

People believe that opal possesses powers of each gemstone whose color appears in its luster, making it a very lucky stone.

PEARL

One of the explanations of the name "pearl" (жемчуг, մարգարիտ) is that it comes from the Latin "pirula" meaning a small pear.

Pearls have been used as decoration for centuries. Greeks believed pearls were tears of gods, while other cultures associated pearls with the moon and called them "teardrops of the moon".

Hindu folklore told that heavenly dewdrops fell into the sea and became pearls.

Two most famous pearls were found in the Gulf of Panama, at around the same time – in the mid-16th century, both by African slaves, who got their freedom as a reward.

European kings and queens owned these pearls for centuries. They were pear-shaped; the first one was a little smaller than the second and was named **La Peregrina**, which means "the Pilgrim" in Spanish. The second one was named **La Pelegrina** – with just one letter different from the first name, to show similarities of the jewels.

The last owner of La Peregrina was Elizabeth Taylor.

La Pelegrina was in possession of Zinaida Yusupova of Saint Petersburg. Her son, Felix Yusupov, after the revolution of 1917, smuggled the pearl out of Russia and sold it in 1953 to a jeweler.

While talking about pearls, we have to mention the **mother-of-pearl** and **abalone**, which is the mother-of-pearl of the abalone shell.

Pearls symbolize purity. They are believed to attract wealth and luck.

PERIDOT

The origin of the name of this gem is unclear. Most scholars agree that the word "peridot" is derived from the Arabic "*faridat*" which means "gem," but some believe it is rooted in the Greek word "*peridona*" meaning "giving plenty."

Perhaps that's why peridot (хризолит, պերիդոտ)is associated with prosperity and good fortune. Peridot is a gem-quality **olivine**.

According to Hawaiian legend, peridot is one of the stones among the small pieces of solidified lava, that are called **Pele's tears**.

In the Hawaiian religion, Pele is the goddess of fire and volcanoes. It is said that her father expelled her from home in Tahiti because of her difficult and hot temper. Pele reached Hawaiian Islands where she created many fiery volcanoes.

One of the many legends that surround goddess Pele, tells about how she met Lohiau, the King of Kauai, and fell in love with him. Unfortunately, he chose her sister over her, and that is the reason for Pele's tears.

People say that Pele often wanders throughout the Hawaiian Islands, especially near volcanic craters and near her home of Kilauea, one of the most active volcanoes in the world, located on the Island of Hawaii.

Sometimes she appears in the guise of a tall, attractive woman, while other times as an ugly old beggar, accompanied by a white dog. Those who are generous with her are rewarded by her but the greedy ones are punished.

As many tourists like to pick up a lava rock, or a beautiful piece of peridot from the beach and take it home as a souvenir, it is also said that Pele curses those who do that. That is why thousands of rocks are mailed daily to Hawaii from travelers over the world who allegedly have suffered bad luck and misfortunes after bringing home Hawaiian rocks.

Ancient Egyptians called peridot the "gem of the sun," believing it protected its wearer from terrors of the night.

PYRITE

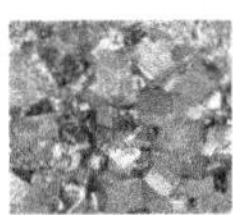

The name "pyrite" (пирит, պիրիտ) is derived from the Greek "*pyrites*", meaning "in fire", because it creates sparks when struck against steel.

Pyrite has a metallic luster and a pale yellow hue, which makes it resemble gold, and is the reason for its nickname "the fool's gold". The well known **marcasite** jewelry is jewelry made not from marcasite but from pyrite.

Marcasite jewelry achieved most popularity in the Victorian era and with more subdued jewelry of Art Nouveau. With the death of her husband, Queen Victoria was in mourning and her entire court was required to wear black and not opulent jewelry, and for that, marcasite jewelry was quite suitable.

Pyrite is considered to be a stone of intellect and mental stability.

QUARTZ

The word "quartz" (кварц, որձաքար) has originated from Slavic word "*tvrdy*" – hard.

Ancient Greeks referred to quartz as "*krustallos*" and believed that quartz is permanently frozen piece of ice. Today, the term **"rock crystal"** (горный хрусталь, բյուրեղապակի) is sometimes used as an alternative name for the purest, colorless form of quartz.

Originally, **rhinestones**, used in jewelry, were rock crystals gathered from the river Rhine. Today, the name rhinestone applies to varieties of crystal glass (lead glass).

Quartz is the second most abundant mineral of the Earth's crust behind **feldspar**. Most of the semi-precious gemstones are in the quartz group. Here are some of them: **amethyst, citrine, rose quartz, milky quartz, smoky quartz, tiger's eye.**

Quartz **druse** (**druzy**) is also common. "Druse" is called multiple tiny crystal coating of a rock surface.

RHODOCHROSITE

The name "rhodochrosite" (родохрозит, ռոդոխռոզիտ) is derived from the Greek word meaning "rose-colored".

Rhodochrosite is considered Argentina's national gemstone. Incas called it the Inca Rose. Here is its legend.

A long time ago, on the island in Lake Titicaca, Peru, there was a temple where the virgin priestesses lived who worshipped their god Inti, and the Sun and the Moon.

The entrance to the temple was prohibited for all men be that a warrior, king or priest. However, one day, brave warrior Tupac dared to enter the temple.

As soon as his eyes saw her, the warrior fell in love with the beautiful Priestess Ñusta, and she fell in love with him. Their love was so great, that they were willing to risk everything they achieved in their lives, and even life itself - only to be together. Therefore, they escaped.

The frustrated Emperor ordered his numerous warriors to find and kill them, but nobody could find the lovers. The couple hid in the mountains and over time had many kids.

In spite of all their love, they weren't able to break the curse that thousands of Inca shamans had cast on them. Soon Ñusta died, and was buried on top of a mountain. Not long after, died Tupac.

Many years passed. A stranger passing by the mountains one afternoon, discovered a tomb with the name of Priestess Ñusta on it.

Surprised, he also noticed stone blood roses around the tombstone. As everybody in the Inca Empire knew the story of the disappeared Priestess and the warrior, he decided to take one of these roses to the Emperor.

When the Emperor received this amazing present and heard where it came from, he became overwhelmed with emotions. All of a sudden, he stopped hating the lovers and pardoned them.

From that moment on, rhodochrosite got the "Inca rose stone" name, and became a symbol of peace, love, and forgiveness.

ROCKS

There are three major groups of rocks on Earth: **igneous**, **sedimentary** and **metamorphic** (магматические, осадочные и метаморфические горные породы) (մագմայական, նստվածքային և փոխակերպային ապարներ).

The name **igneous** comes from the Latin "igneus" meaning "fire". Igneous rocks are formed through the cooling of magma or lava. Examples of such rocks include **granite** and **basalt**; **feldspars** and **quartz** are present in igneous rocks. **Sedimentary** rocks are formed by the accumulation of fragments of earlier rocks and organic particles, like, for example, fragments of corals or mollusks. Examples of sedimentary rocks are **limestone** and **sandstone** (famous Antelope Canyon, USA, was formed by erosion of Navajo Sandstone). The name **metamorphic** comes from the Greek words "meta"- change and "morphe"- form. Metamorphic rocks are formed by subjecting any rock type to different temperature and pressure conditions than those in which the original rock was formed. **Marble** is an example of a metamorphic rock.

RUBY

The name "ruby" (рубин, սուտակ) comes from "*rubeus*", the Latin word for red. In ancient Sanskrit, ruby translated to "*ratnaraj*", which means "king of precious stones."

Rubies have been treasured throughout history, particularly in Asian countries. They were traded along China's North Silk Road as early as 200 B.C. Chinese noblemen decorated their armor with rubies because they believed the gem would grant protection. They also buried rubies beneath building foundations to secure good fortune.

Hindus regard ruby as more valuable than any other gemstone. They have a mythical, wish fulfilling spiritual tree Kalpa (Kalpavriksha), which is inhabited by the god Shiva. This tree is often described as growing upside down and made of sapphires, diamonds, topazes, emeralds, and other gems, while most important part of the tree, the fruits, are of rubies. The more they ripen the redder they become (read Comments on p.55 to learn more about rubies).

Ancient Hindus believed that "He who worships Krishna with big rubies will be reborn as a powerful emperor. If with a small ruby, he will be born a king". In Hindu folklore, the glowing fire within rubies burned so hot that they were able to boil water.

The Greek legends similarly claimed that ruby's warmth could melt wax.

In Burma, warriors believed that rubies made them invincible. They even implanted rubies into their skin to get protection in battle.

According to Burmese legend, there once existed a gigantic serpent-dragon, Naga. This Naga laid three eggs. From the first, hatched the King of Burma. From the second egg emerged the Emperor of China, and from the third one came a magical seed from which all the rubies in the world originated.

In another folktale, a fisherman and his wife found an egg and placed it in a nearby pond. The egg hatched into a crocodile. The couple fed the crocodile every day until one day crocodile ate the husband.

The fisherman-husband was reincarnated as a magician who wanted revenge against the thankless beast. By that time the crocodile was reincarnated as a human.

The fisherman-turned-magician struck the water three times with his magic wand and the crocodile-turned-human appeared before the magician, who killed him. However, as the crocodile-turned-human died, he was reincarnated as a crocodile once again but this time the part of his body that was in the water was turned into rubies.

Ruby is believed to boost your energy and promote high esteem, intuition and spiritual wisdom.

SAPPHIRE

The name "sapphire" (сапфир, շափյուղա) comes from the Greek word *"sappheiros"*, meaning "blue stone".

Some believe it originated from the Sanskrit word *"sanipriya"* which meant "dear to Saturn."

The deep blue color of the sapphire looks like a cloudless night sky, and ancients believed that the world was set upon an enormous sapphire.

There is also a legend that Prometheus was the first one to wear a blue sapphire ring. According to the well known myth, by the order of Zeus, Prometheus was chained to a mountain, as a punishment for stealing fire from gods and giving it to humans.

To torture him, a giant eagle would fly and eat his liver every day and by night it will grow back again. When Hercules came to rescue Prometheus of this torment, he broke the chains and only a link of it stayed on Prometheus' finger. Attached to the link was a blue stone, a sapphire.

Though sapphires are typically blue, they also come in **yellow**, **purple**, **orange** and **green** colors.

Greeks wore sapphire for guidance when seeking answers from the oracle. Buddhists believed it brought spiritual enlightenment, and Hindus used it during worship. Early Christian kings cherished sapphire's powers of protection by using it in religious rings.

Ancient Hebrews believed that the Ten Commandments were engraved on tablets of sapphire, though historians now believe the blue stone referenced in the Bible may have been **lapis lazuli**.

People attach symbolic meaning to the three white lines across the star sapphire. They say that they represent faith, hope and destiny, and would protect the owner even after the stone was no longer in the owner's possession (read Comments on p.55 to learn more about star sapphires).

SELENITE

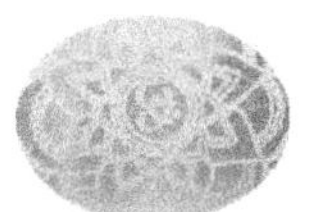

The name (селенит, սելէն) comes from the Greek word meaning "stone of the moon". Selenite is a variety of **gypsum**, very soft mineral, that could be scratched with a fingernail.

There are four "crystalline" varieties of gypsum: selenite, **satin spar, desert rose** and **gypsum flower**. They are often grouped together and called **selenite**.

Selenite itself is most often transparent and colorless.

It is believed to protect pregnancy and motherhood.

SERPENTINE

The name "serpentine" (серпентин, սերպենտին) came from the **greenish** color of the stone reminding of a serpent.

The high grade serpentine was known as "false **jade**", and was very popular among Indian craftsmen.

Serpentinite marbles are also widely used.

Serpentine is said to attract love and money.

SPINEL

The name "spinel" (шпинель, շպինել) comes from the Latin "*spina*", meaning "arrow", possibly because of its sharp edged crystals.

Spinel comes in various colors: **red**, **pink**, **blue**, **violet**, **dark green**, **brown**, **black**, colorless. Rose-tinted spinel was known as "**balas ruby**", the violet one - "**eastern amethyst**".

The most famous spinels are **The Black Prince's Ruby** and **Timur Ruby** from the British Crown Jewels, in exposition in the Jewel House at the Tower of London, and the **Samarian Spinel**. Here are their stories.

The Black Prince's Ruby is a large red cabochon spinel. In the 14th century, it was given to the so-called Black Prince, Prince of Wells, who was expected to become the King of England.

Before that, the spinel was known to be in the possession of the Moorish Prince of Granada. Granada was under continuous attacks by Christians, and the Moorish Prince was ready to surrender to the King of Castile Don Pedro the Cruel. Don Pedro arranged a meeting with the Prince of Granada, but when they met, he ordered to kill the Prince's servants and then personally stabbed the Prince.

When Moorish Prince's corpse was searched, the spinel was found and Don Pedro took ownership of it.

After some time though, Don Pedro had to part with the spinel, and give it to the Black Prince as a payment for his support in putting down revolt.

Since then, the Black Prince's Ruby adorned at first helmets and then crowns of the British royalty.

The Timur Ruby is an unfaceted, polished red spinel, thought to be a ruby until 1851.

It is inscribed with the names and dates of its previous owners.

British took possession of the Timur Ruby and **Koh-i-Noor** diamond after conquering Punjab, India in 1849. Then, they were both presented to Queen Victoria.

The Samarian Spinel is one of the largest gemstones and is part of the Iranian Crown Jewels. It was captured by the Persian King during the 18th century conquest of India. The Samarian Spinel has a hole in it, and a diamond was added later to conceal the hole.

Spinel is believed to help bring in energy, eliminate forgetfulness, and attract money and wealth.

TANZANITE

Tanzanite (танзанит, տանձանիթ) was discovered in 1967 in Tanzania, not far from the mount Kilimanjaro. Hence the name.

Tanzania mines are the only source of tanzanite. It is used as relatively cheap gemstone to substitute sapphire after undergoing heat treatment to get more sapphire like color.

The stone was named and advertised by Tiffany & Co. Its popularity increased due to use of tanzanite jewelry by famous actress Elizabeth Taylor.

Tanzanite is considered to be a calming gemstone.

TOPAZ

The name "topaz" (топаз, սպագիոն) derives from "*Topazios*", the ancient Greek name for St. John's Island in the Red Sea. Although the yellow stones, famously mined there, were probably not topaz, it soon became the name for most **yellowish** stones.

Russia's Ural Mountains became a leading source of topaz in the 19th century. There is a prized **pinkish-orange** gemstone from those mines that was named Imperial Topaz to honor the Russian Czar.

Topaz can also be **colorless**, **blue**, or **purple**.

One famous colorless giant, egg shaped topaz found in Brazil, for a long time was thought to be the largest diamond in the world. It belonged to the king of Portugal and was called **Braganza Diamond**, by the name of the royal family. Brazil is one of the largest producers of topaz.

There is also a known **"mystic"** topaz. It is not a gem type, but rather a colorless topaz treated in special way. Since the treatment is a coating, topaz is not permanently enhanced, but, while the coating lasts, it produces kaleidoscope of colors. Same is true for other "mystic" gems.

Topaz is believed to solve mysteries, give women beauty and sobriety to men.

TOURMALINE

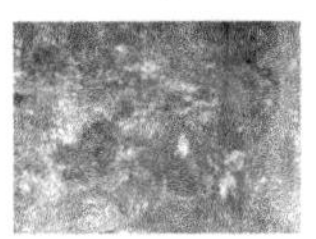

The name "tourmaline." (турмалин, տուրմալին) comes from the Sinhalese words *"tura mali"*, which mean "stone of mixed colors."

An ancient Egyptian legend says that as the stone tourmaline traveled its long journey from the heart of the Earth up towards the Sun, it traveled along a rainbow and collected all the colors of the rainbow along the way, and this is why tourmaline comes in almost every color.

The ability of this stone to look like other gemstones led to some confusion.

For example, many gemstones in the Russian Crown jewels from the 17th century which were once thought to be **rubies** are in fact tourmalines.

In South America, green tourmaline is still called the "**Brazilian emerald**".

Tourmaline also occurs in combinations of two or three colors.

Sometimes the colors are at different ends of the crystal, while other times one color is in the heart of the crystal and another on the outside. When the later combination displays a **pink** center with a **green** rind, it is called "**watermelon tourmaline**".

Magicians used black tourmaline as a talisman to protect against negative energy and evil forces.

Today, many still believe that it can shield against radiation, pollutants, toxins and damaging thoughts.

TURQUOISE

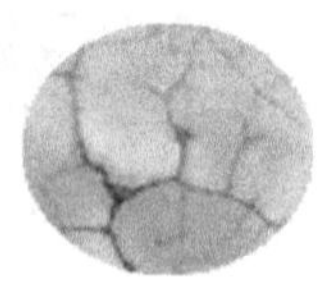

The word turquoise (бирюза, փիրուզ) dates back to the 13th century, coming from the French expression "*pierre tourques*", which refers to the "Turkish stone".

Russian and Armenian names come from the Persian "*firooze*" meaning "luck bringing stone" or from "*pirooz*" – "the winner".

Ancient Persia (now Iran) was the traditional source for **sky blue** turquoise. Today this color is often called "Persian blue", regardless of its origin.

The Sinai Peninsula in Egypt was also an important historical source of turqoise.

The U.S. is now the world's largest turquoise supplier. Nevada, New Mexico, California and Colorado produce turquoise, but Arizona leads in production by value, as well as quality. This stone is a staple in Native American jewelry.

There is a Native American legend about a chief with skin the color of turquoise. One day, he was running from his enemies through the hot desert.

Whenever he stopped to rest, beads of his sweat fell to the ground. Rocks that collected the sweat of the chief became turquoise.

In many cultures turquoise was considered as a holy stone, a bringer of good fortune and protection.

While in ancient times the color change of stones was regarded as a threat to the well-being of the owner, now we know that change of color of turquoise can be caused by light, dust and other factors.

ZIRCON

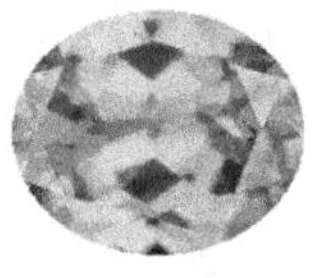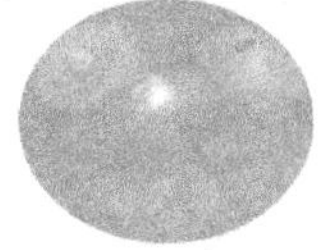

The name "zircon" (циркон, ցիրկոն) likely comes from the Persian word "*zargun*", meaning "gold-colored."

Other assumption is that the word originated from the Arabic "*zarkun*", meaning "scarlet red." Given natural range of colors of zircon – colorless, **red, orange, yellow, green, blue** and **brown** – both explanations make sense.

For many years, colorless specimens were popular substitute for diamonds. They were called "**Matura diamonds**" by the name of the town in Ceylon. Moreover, when gem dealers discovered that heating cinnamon-colored zircons makes them permanently colorless and more brilliant, zircon became known as the "**poor man's diamond**".

Another stone that is regarded as a diamond alternative is **moissanite**—discovered my H. Moissan. Moissanite can be natural or lab created.

Zircon is different from **cubic zirconia**, which is a synthetic, lab-created stone. The technique of single-crystal growth of cubic zirconia was perfected by Soviet scientists of the Physical Institute of Academy of Sciences (FIAN—acronym of the Institute in Russian). They named the product **fianit**. Its commercial production began in 1976. But the name fianit for cubic zirconia is used only in the former Soviet Union.

Jacinth is an **orange-red** transparent variety of zircon. The name is derived from the hyacinth flower, the wild variety of which has the same hue. It is a very rare and valued by the jewelers gemstone.

Zircon is believed to be a highly spiritual stone, which will help you to love yourself and others, act more effectively and achieve your goals.

HIGH PRIEST AARON'S BREASTPLATE

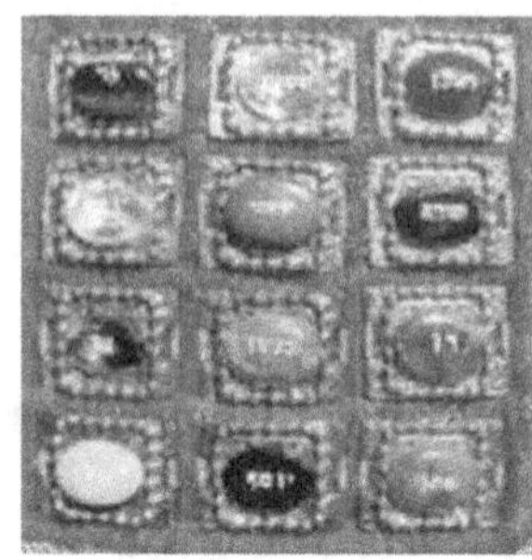

Following the tradition of lapidaries - books about precious and semi-precious stones, I want to mention High Priest Aaron's breastplate with 12 gemstones on it.

It has four rows, with three jewels in each. Twelve gemstones stand for 12 tribes of Israel. Their names were engraved on the stones. It is said that Moses used **Shamir worm** to do the work (read Lapis Lazuli part to see how this worm was used by King Solomon).

The names were first traced in ink, and then Shamir worm passed over the stones, engraving the inscriptions. No particles of the gems were removed in the procedure, which points on the magical essence of the process.

As a result, the breastplate was thought to have supernatural powers. They say that it was able to reveal guilt – if the name of a guilty person was pronounced, the stones of the breastplate would lose their luster and become dim.

Jews believed that the stones in the High Priest's Breastplate carry emblematic meaning. In the book of Revelation, these stones are described as the foundation stones of the New Jerusalem.

Absence of **diamond** among the jewels of the breastplate is explained by two reasons. First, that it was very costly to get a diamond that big, and second that it would have marked too great of a distinction between the tribe symbolized by diamond and the rest of the tribes, which was not desirable.

The exact stones that were used on the breastplate, are still a mystery.

There were supposedly two breastplates: the Breastplate of Aaron and the Breastplate of the Second Temple separated from each other by an interval of eight centuries. Here are the stones used in them, according to their position:

The Breastplate of Aaron	The Breastplate of the Second Temple
Red jasper	Carnelian
Light-green serpentine	Peridot
Green feldspar	Emerald
Almandine garnet	Ruby
Lapis-lazuli	Lapis-lazuli
Onyx	Onyx
Brown agate	Sapphire or jacinth
Banded agate	Banded agate
Amethyst	Amethyst
Yellow jasper	Topaz
Malachite	Beryl
Green jasper or jade	Green jasper or jade

BIRTHSTONES

In the Middle Ages, twelve gemstones of the Breastplate were connected with twelve apostles, and each apostle was associated with one of the twelve months of the calendar. As of today, different cultures have different lists of gemstones corresponding to the person's month of birth.

In this table all of them are combined, so you can choose, using your intuition, which birthstone works better for you.

Month	Gemstone
January	Garnet
February	Amethyst, Hyacinth, Pearl
March	Aquamarine, Bloodstone, Jasper
April	Diamond, Sapphire, Rock Crystal
May	Emerald, Agate, Chrysoprase
June	Alexandrite, Pearl, Moonstone, Cat's Eye, Turquoise, Agate
July	Ruby, Turquoise, Onyx, Carnelian, Sapphire
August	Peridot, Sardonyx, Carnelian, Moonstone, Topaz, Ruby, Spinel
September	Sapphire, Chrysolite, Lapis Lazuli, Zircon
October	Tourmaline, Opal, Aquamarine, Tourmaline, Coral
November	Topaz, Pearl, Citrine, Cat's Eye
December	Bloodstone, Turquoise, Ruby, Lapis Lazuli, Zircon, Tanzanite

Wearing of the appropriate zodiac gem was always believed to strengthen the influence of the **zodiac sign** on those born under it.

It is said that fashion of natal rings came either from Poland or from Germany in the 18th century.

There are different versions of correspondence of birthstones to the zodiac signs. Here is one of them:

Dates	Zodiac Signs		Stones
21 Jan. – 18 Feb.	**Aquarius** (Водолей, Ջրհոս)	♒	**Garnet**
19 Feb.– 20 Mar.	**Pisces** (Рыбы, Ձկներ)	♓	**Amethyst**
21 Mar. – 20 Apr.	**Aries** (Овен, Խոյ)	♈	**Bloodstone**
21 Apr. – 21 May	**Taurus** (Телец, Ցուլ)	♉	**Sapphire**
22 May – 21 June	**Gemini** (Близнецы, Երկվորյակներ)	♊	**Agate**
21 June – 22 July	**Cancer** (Рак, Խեցգետին)	♋	**Emerald**
23 July – 22 Aug.	**Leo** (Лев, Առյուծ)	♌	**Onyx**
23 Aug. – 22 Sep.	**Virgo** (Дева, Կույս)	♍	**Carnelian**
23 Sep. – 23 Oct.	**Libra** (Весы, Կշեռք)	♎	**Chrysolite**
24 Oct. – 21 Nov.	**Scorpio** (Скорпион, Կարիճ)	♏	**Beryl**
22 Nov. – 21 Dec.	**Sagittarius** (Стрелец, Աղեղնավոր)	♐	**Topaz**
22 Dec. – 21 Jan.	**Capricorn** (Козерог, Այծեղջյուր)	♑	**Ruby**

THE STONES AND ROCKS OF ARMENIA

Armenia is often called "The Stone Land", "*Karastan*", «Քարաստան».

The major part of Armenian stones have volcanic origin.

Gemstones that are found in Armenia are **obsidian, carnelian, jasper, agate, onyx, jade, turquoise, quartz, rhodonite, malachite, chalcedony** .

Here are the most common rocks of Armenia:

Basalt (բազալտ)

The word "basalt" is ultimately derived from the **Latin** *"basaltes"*, a misspelling of Latin *"basanites"* word meaning "very hard stone".

In Armenia, you can see basalt or, as people call it, "mountain stone" everywhere. Basalt rocks often take the form of regular columns leaving impression that they are manmade. Many examples of these "handmade" rocks are located in the gorge of river Hrazdan and in Geghard.

Granite (գրանիտ)

The word "granite" comes from the Latin *"granum"*, meaning "grain", because of the coarse-grained structure of the rock. Armenia has more than 50 granite mines.

Marble (մարմար)

The word "marble" derives from the Greek *"marmaron"* with the meaning "crystalline rock, shining stone". Armenia is very rich of high quality marble.

Obsidian (վանական, օբսիդիան, հրաբխային ապակի)

Armenian name "vanakat" comes from the fact that obsidian in Armenia was first found in the region of Van Lake.

Perlite (պեռլիտ)

Perlite is a volcanic glass. The name comes from the French word *"perle"* meaning "pearl". While the crude rock can be black, perlite, after heat treatment, acquires color from snowy to grayish white. Hence the name.

Pumice (пемза, պեմզա)

The name originated from Latin "*spuma*" meaning "foam". Light weightiness of pumice was used in constructions as far back as Roman times.

Tuff (տուֆ)

The name "tuff" originated from Italian "*tufo*" meaning "porous rock". There are 5 kinds of Armenian tuff – the tuff from Ani, which has yellowish-orange color, tuff from Artik (with pink and violet colors), from Yerevan (black and red colored), from Burakan (colored in pink or brown with black lines) and a tuff that has mix pattern color. Almost all these kinds of tuff are represented in the buildings of Yerevan, the capital of Armenia.

THE DRAGON STONES

The Dragon Stones, "*vishapakarer*", (вишапы, драконовые камни, վիշապաքարեր) are menhirs (the word comes from Brittonic language, "*men*" means "stone" and "*hir*" means "long", and the name is used for standing stones).

Armenian Dragon Stones are mostly in the shape of fish, with pictures of animals, water, and are usually erected by the lakes, springs, wells or other water reservoirs.

Allegedly, they are idols of gods of water and agriculture.

KARAHUNGE

Not far from the city of Sisian is located Karahunge (Քարահունջ): megalithic structure, allegedly the oldest observatory in the world. Until about the year of 1990, it was known by the name "Powerful Stones" (Зорац-карер, Զորաց քարեր).

Karahunge is considered to be about 7500 years old.

Megalith is a large natural stone used in constructions. The name comes from the Greek "*megas*" meaning "great", and "*lithos*" meaning "stone". The word "megalithic" describes structures made of such large stones. **Stonehenge** in the UK, is one of the world's best-known megalithic structures, which is believed to be constructed in about 3000 BC.

The stones of Karahunge are of basalt and were lifted up from the local Dar river.

Many of the stones have holes in them, which is very rare in the ancient monuments of this kind.

KHACHKARS

The Armenian word "*khachkar*" (хачкар, крест-камень, խաչքար) means "cross-stone".

Khachkars are characteristics of Medieval Christian Armenian art.

It is a memorial stone with a carved cross on it with additional motifs such as rosettes (a round flower design), elaborate patterns, grapes, pomegranates.

Usually the cross is carved above the rosette or solar disc. Sometimes there is also a cornice – horizontal molding that crowns the khachkar.

Most khachkars were placed in cemeteries, for salvation of the soul of the deceased person. Besides that, they were erected to commemorate a military victory, or to protect from natural disasters.

First khachkars appeared in the 9th century. The peak of their carving was in the 12-14th centuries.

COMMENTS

About the Orlov Diamond

In the middle of the 20th century researchers found archives proving different story of the Orlov diamond.

According to them, **Empress Catherine II** saw the diamond, loved it and decided to get it for herself. However, she didn't want people to know that she used a large amount of money from the meagre government account for her personal pleasures. To hide this, she asked Hovhannes Lazaryan (**Ivan Lazarev**, one of the founders of the Lazarev Institute of Oriental Languages in Moscow; nowadays its building is used for Armenian Embassy), who was at the time in a high position of royal jeweler, to present the diamond as a gift from Count Orlov. And that he did.

Aventurine

Like the meaning of the name itself ("aventurine" is derived from the Italian "*a ventura*" meaning "by chance") just by chance, after this book was already composed, I encountered jewelry made from **aventurine**, and decided to get some more information about this rock.

It turned out to be very interesting.

At first, somewhere in the 17th century, **aventurine glass**, also known as **goldstone**, was unexpectedly created "by chance" by alchemists. It was man made and had starry internal reflections.

Much later, a natural stone with similar glittering effect was discovered and called aventurine. Aventurine comes in a form of **quartz**, which has shimmering effect called **aventurescence**. Stones may be **green**, **orange**, **brown**, **yellow**, **blue** or **gray**.

Aventurine also may be in a form of **feldspar**, with the same shimmering, glittering effect, and in that case it is called **sunstone**.

Sunstones were mentioned since 13th-14th centuries in Iceland and allegedly were used as navigation instruments. According to the medieval literature, sunstones were used for location of sun in an overcast sky.

Corundum

Corundum is the hardest mineral after diamond, best known for its gem quality varieties— ruby and sapphire. Ruby is the **red** variety, while sapphire includes all other colors: **blue**, **colorless**, **gray**, **brown**, **yellow**, **green**, **violet**.

Star Sapphire

The star sapphire is a sapphire that exhibits a star-like phenomenon, called *asterism*, when a six-rayed star pattern appears if stone is viewed with a single overhead light source.

The largest star sapphire was discovered in 2015 in Sri Lanka. It has blue color and is called **The Star of Adam**.

The name was given by its current owner as a reference to the belief of some Muslims and Christians in Sri Lanka that the original Garden of Eden was located in Sri Lanka, and when Adam was exiled from Eden, he set his foot on the conical mountain in the center of the country and left his footprint there.

This mountain is known by the names of Adam's Peak and Sri Pada "sacred footprint" as Buddhists believe it to hold the footprint of Buddha and Hindus—the footprint of Shiva.

Before the discovery of the Star of Adam, **The Black Star of Queensland** was considered to be the largest star sapphire. It is a black sapphire which was found by a 12 year old boy in the mid 1930, in Australia.

Not realizing the value of the stone, the family used it as a doorstop in their home for over a decade, until the father, Harry Spencer, who was a miner, took a closer look at it and discovered the gem hidden within.

In 1947 he sold the stone to Armenian jeweler **Harry Kazanjian**, who cut it into the famous 733 carat Black Star of Queensland, revealing the six pointed star.

The stone brought its owners good luck and their business boomed.

For some time the gem was loaned to the **Smithsonian Natural History Museum** for exposition but eventually was sold to a private collector, with the proceeds funding scholarship programs at the Gemological Institute of America (GIA).

About the Carat and Karat

In the book about stones, it is appropriate to mention carat and karat. The **carat**, symbol ct, is a unit of mass equal to 200mg and is used for measuring gemstones.

The word "carat" comes from the Greek word meaning "carob seed". Throughout history, carob tree seed was used as a unit of weight to measure jewelry.

The **karat** (not carat), symbol K or kt, is a measure of purity of gold alloys.

For example, 24 karat gold is considered pure, 18 karat gold is 18 parts gold (75%) and 6 parts another metal and so on.

Many European countries instead of karat, use so called "decimal hallmark stamps".

For example, if in the USA and UK they say that it is 18 karat gold, it is equivalent to 75% of pure gold mass in the alloy and could be represented by '750' hallmark stamp.

Acknowledgements

I want to thank my daughter Vera, for taking time and editing this book, and my daughter Bella, for allowing me to use her art in the book design.

INDEX

Z

Zircon 5,45
Zodiac Signes 49